AFTERLIFE

By
Tracy Ogali

with illustrations by students from
Chestnut Grove Academy

Clink
Street

London | New York

Published by Clink Street Publishing 2016

Copyright © 2016

First edition.

ISBN: 978-1-909477-81-0
E-Book: 978-1-909477-82-7

Dedication

For Kayne and Mya

and to all those I have loved and lost

my mum, my dad, and my husband

- my biggest contributors.

THIS JOURNEY BEGINS AT THE START OF AN END,
THE LOSS OF A PARENT, A FATHER, A FRIEND....
IN A HOLE, ON A HILL BY THE TALLEST TREE
LIVES A YOUNG RED FOX WITH HIS FAMILY.

THIS ONCE BRIGHT FOX HAS LOST HIS WAY
DEVASTATED SINCE THAT FATEFUL DAY.
CONSUMED BY SHOCK, IN COMPLETE DENIAL,
REFUSING TO ACCEPT THIS END WAS FINAL.

"THIS DOESN'T MAKE SENSE," FOX CRIED OUT.
"WHY HAS THIS HAPPENED? WHAT'S IT ABOUT?"
MOTHER EXPLAINED, "ALTHOUGH HE HAS GONE,
HIS SPIRIT WILL CONTINUE AND ALWAYS LIVE ON."

WHAT THAT MEANT FOX WASN'T TOO SURE
HIS SPIRIT ALIVE! IT SEEMED TOO OBSCURE.
HE ASKS HIS MOTHER "WHY DID HE DIE?
HE LEFT ME ALONE, I NEED TO KNOW WHY?

"I HAVE NO PURPOSE, AMBITION OR MEANING.
NO LIFE, NO FUTURE FOR ME TO BELIEVE IN.

I WANT TO WAKE UP FROM THIS BAD DREAM,
A CONSTANT NIGHTMARE FAR TOO EXTREME."

HIS MOTHER REASSURED "THINGS WILL TAKE TIME."
FOX JUST SAW A HUGE MOUNTAIN TO CLIMB.
DAYS PASSING BY IN TICKS AND TOCKS,
EACH ONE A STRUGGLE FOR OUR YOUNG RED FOX.

HE REGURGITATES THE PAST, WHAT IT WAS ABOUT,
TO CHANGE, IMPROVE, OR COMPLETELY RUB OUT.
MANY WEEKS WENT BY WITH A GROWING IDEA,
A PLAN WAS SLOWLY BEGINNING TO APPEAR.

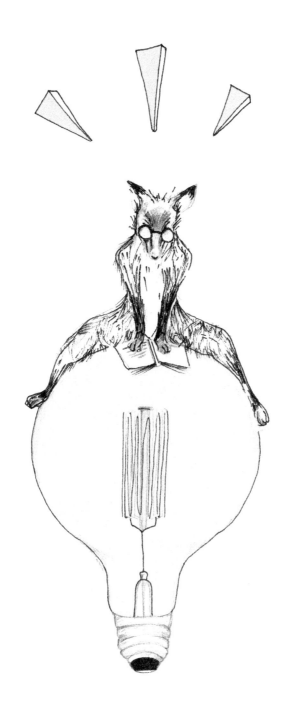

"I NEED TO UNDERSTAND THE REASON WHY
WE ARE BORN TO LIVE BUT THEN WE DIE"
FOX WORKED ON HIS PLAN OVER SOME TIME.
MAYBE RIDICULOUS OR MAYBE SUBLIME!

"WHO WILL PROVIDE ME WITH THE ASSISTANCE?
ABOUT LIFE AND DEATH AND ALL IN EXISTENCE?"
WHAT WOULD HE LEARN? WHAT WOULD HE SEE?
HE HAD EXPECTATIONS OF HOW IT WOULD BE.

HE DREAMT OF MEETING PHILOSOPHERS AND PREACHERS,
SHAMANS, MONKS AND ALL THE WISE CREATURES.
ALCHEMISTS, THINKERS, REALISTS, MAGICIANS.
SHARING IN KNOWLEDGE AND ANCIENT TRADITIONS.

APPREHENSIVE TO LEAVE HIS FAMILY BEHIND
BUT COMPELLED TO SEE WHAT HE COULD FIND.
WHILST HE WAS YOUNG, STILL ONLY A YOUTH,
FOX SAID, "IT'S TIME TO SEARCH FOR THE TRUTH."

PREPARED TO GO TO THE ENDS OF THE EARTH
TO FIND MEANING IN DEATH AND REASON FOR BIRTH.
FOX SAYS HIS GOODBYES TO SET OUT ALONE,
TOWARDS THE PATH, DESTINATION? UNKNOWN.

WITH HIS COMPASS FOX SETS FORTH ON HIS QUEST,
TO FOLLOW THE SUN FROM THE EAST TO THE WEST.
SPRING WAS APPROACHING, THE EMERGENCE OF NEW;
HE STOOD ON THE MOUNTAIN ABSORBING THE VIEW.

FOX TRAVELLED FOR MILES OBSERVING MOTHER NATURE
WONDROUSLY CHANGING HER NATURAL BEHAVIOUR.
HER BEAUTY, HER POWER A FRAGILE SIMPLICITY,
TENDER, YET HARSH IN ALL HER COMPLEXITY.

MEANDERING THE FOREST, CLIMBING HILLS AND ROCKS.
ENCOUNTERING NO CREATURES, NOT EVEN A FOX!
HE MET A FEW ANIMALS THAT OFFERED DIRECTIONS.
BUT NONE HAD ANSWERS TO ANY OF HIS QUESTIONS.

THROUGH WIND, HIGH SEAS, DESERT AND SNOW
DOUBT SET IN, WOULD ANYONE KNOW?
EVENTUALLY HE FOUND THE CREATURES NEEDED,
THEY OFFERED THEIR WISDOM, HAD HE SUCCEEDED?

HE ASKED AN EAGLE, HYENA, CHAMELEON, DOLPHIN,
A LION, AN ELEPHANT, AN OWL AND A PENGUIN.
THE QUESTIONS POSED WERE ALWAYS THE SAME.
DOES LIFE HAVE A PURPOSE, A MEANING, OR AIM?

THE EAGLE RECOMMENDED WORSHIPPING THE SUN.
THE HYENA DECLARED TO LAUGH AND HAVE FUN.
THE DOLPHIN PROPOSED TO DANCE TO THE MOON.
THE LION KEEP FIT AND YOUR BODY IN TUNE.

THE ELEPHANT PROCLAIMED HAVING NO INTERFERENCE.
THE CHAMELEON ADVISED TO CHANGE HIS APPEARANCE.

THE OWL ENCOURAGED GETTING A GOOD EDUCATION.
THE PENGUIN URGED TO STUDY EACH CONSTELLATION.

WITH ANSWERS A PLENTY FOX WENT ON A MISSION,
TO PRACTISE THE GUIDANCE, TO FIND DEFINITION.
HE WORSHIPPED THE SUN, DANCED TO THE MOON,
STUDIED THE SKIES, JOINED A LEARNING COMMUNE.

HE SHAVED OFF HIS COAT, LIVED LIKE A MONK,
GAINED A SENSE OF HUMOUR, NEVER ATE JUNK.

AS SEASONS WENT BY NOTHING WAS HAPPENING.
"I'M SO FRUSTRATED FROM ALL OF THIS PRACTISING.

"I'M NO LION, NOR OWL, I'M SIMPLY A FOX
I NEED A SOLUTION OUTSIDE OF THE BOX!
I'VE SEARCHED SO LONG, I STILL DON'T KNOW
THE MEANING TO LIFE, IT'S TIME TO LET GO."

THROUGH THE WINTER, SPRING, SUMMER AND FALL,
FOX TRAVELS HOME TO THE TREE THAT IS TALL.
THE JOURNEY BACK HOME WAS REALLY QUITE TOUGH,
HE FELT LIKE A FAILURE; HE'D NOT DONE ENOUGH.

AROUND THE GLOBE, HE'D EXPLORED AND SEEN;
DIFFICULT TO RETURN TO HIS USUAL ROUTINE.
THE BIGGEST QUESTION HE PONDERED UPON:
WHY THIS HAD HAPPENED, HOW TO MOVE ON.

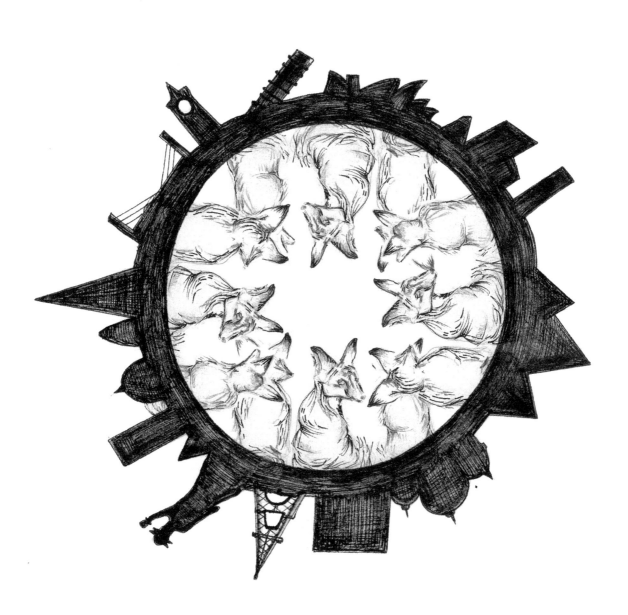

FOX ARRIVED BACK TO THE JOY OF FAMILY,
BACK TO SQUARE ONE, BACK TO NORMALITY.
ON THE HIGHEST HILL BY THE TALLEST TREE
FOX SITS THINKING HOW LIFE SHOULD BE.

THE FEELINGS RETURNED OF THAT FATEFUL DAY
WHEN HE WATCHED HIS FATHER PASS AWAY.
LOCKED AWAY IN THE BACK OF HIS MIND
THOUGHTS OF HIS LOSS WOULD ALWAYS REWIND.

CARRIED AROUND THROUGHOUT HIS QUEST,
HIDDEN AWAY AND NEVER ADDRESSED.
"WHAT IS THE MEANING OF DEATH? FORGET AND LET GO?
WHERE CAN I FIND ANSWERS? DOES ANYONE KNOW?"

FOX WAS SHOUTING LOUDER THAN BEFORE.
HE RAISED HIS VOICE AND BEGAN TO SHOUT MORE.

"WHY AM I HERE? WHY DID HE DIE?

WHAT IS MY PURPOSE? PLEASE,
WHO AM I?

"WHAT'S THE POINT IN SHOUTING?" FOX FELT DEFEATED
"MY SEARCH FOR MEANING WILL NEVER BE COMPLETED.
I JUST NEED TO KNOW WHY MY FUTURE'S UNCLEAR."
OUT OF THE BLUE CAME A WHISPER IN HIS EAR.

WINKING THROUGH SUNLIGHT UP TOWARDS THE SKY,
LANDING ON HIS SNOUT A MAGNIFICENT BUTTERFLY.
"where there is a will there is a way."
IN THE SAME FAINT WHISPER HE HEARD HER SAY.

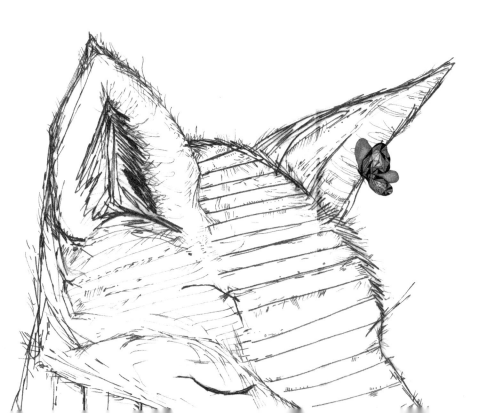

"IS THERE REALLY A WAY?" FOX REPLIES.
"YOU ARE A FOX. SHARP, CUNNING AND WISE."
FOX NEVER CONSIDERED HIMSELF WISE AT ALL.
"SINCE I'VE COME BACK I FEEL LIKE A FOOL.

"I SEARCHED THE WORLD TO DISCOVER MY FATE,
I DIDN'T FIND ANSWERS, I FEAR IT'S TOO LATE."
BUTTERFLY FLUTTERS AND FLOATS TO FLY.
"I UNDERSTAND BUT YOU MUST STILL TRY.

"CREATURES SAY, BETTER LATE THEN NEVER,
IF YOU WANT ANSWERS LET'S SEARCH TOGETHER."
FOX WAS SURPRISED BY HER CONCERN AND REPLY.
IN A SPLIT SECOND HE SAID, "YES BUTTERFLY.

"I'LL TRY ANYTHING; MAYBE YOU'RE MY ANGEL!
IF YOU HELP ME I WOULD BE SO GRATEFUL."
BUTTERFLY WAS FLOATING UP CIRCLING AROUND
FOX HEARD HER SPEAK, A LOW CALMING SOUND.

"TOMORROW HERE BENEATH THE TREE,
AT THE BREAK OF DAWN, I'LL SET YOU FREE."
FOX WAS INTRIGUED IN COMPLETE FASCINATION
EAGER TO ACCEPT HER KIND INVITATION.

"FREE? WHAT DO YOU MEAN?" FOX ASKED.
BUTTERFLY WHISPERED, "FREE FROM THE PAST."
THEN SHE FLEW UP TOWARDS THE SKY.
FOX HADN'T THE CHANCE TO SAY GOODBYE.

FOX SAT WAITING ON THE HILL BY THE TREE,
WOULD THIS BUTTERFLY AT LAST BE THE KEY?
IN THE TWILIGHT OF DAWN THE SUN BEGAN RISING.
FOX FROM A DISTANCE SAW HER ARRIVING.

THROUGH HUES OF RED WITH FINITE PRECISION
ABOVE FIELDS OF FLOWERS A BUTTERFLY'S VISION.
BEFORE SHE DESCENDS TOWARDS THE GROUND
HE HEARS HER VOICE IN A WHISPERING SOUND.

"THE DEATH OF YOUR FATHER FEEL NO BLAME.
LET IT GO, THAT'S YOUR NUMBER ONE AIM!"
FOX WAS CONFUSED, HOW DID SHE KNOW?
HE FELT A STRANGE FEELING, HE BEGAN TO LET GO.

FOX CRUMBLED, FOR THE FIRST TIME HE CRIED,
HE LET GO OF THE GRIEF HE HAD HIDDEN INSIDE.
"I STOOD AND WATCHED AS HE PASSED AWAY
THERE WAS NOTHING I COULD DO OR SAY.

"I DON'T UNDERSTAND! HE WASN'T ILL.
HE FELL DOWN NEXT TO ME, HERE ON THE HILL.
I FEEL GUILTY I SHOULD HAVE DONE MORE,
THIS IS THE PROBLEM I FAIL TO IGNORE.

"I MISS HIM! MY TEACHER AND MY FATHER,
WHATEVER THE QUESTION HE HAD THE ANSWER.
I JUST WANT TO TELL HIM WHAT WAS UNSAID,
I WON'T GET THE CHANCE BECAUSE HE IS DEAD."

SHE ALLOWED FOX TO GRIEVE, THEN SHE STIRRED,
FLYING CLOSE TO HIS EAR, SO SHE WAS HEARD.
"YOUR FATHER TAUGHT YOU HOW TO STAY ALIVE,
THE WAYS OF THE LAND AND HOW TO SURVIVE.

YOU HAVE THE FOUNDATIONS TO CARRY ON,
HE'LL BE BY YOUR SIDE, KEEPING YOU STRONG.
ALL THE GOOD MEMORIES YOU NEED TO REMEMBER;
NEGATIVE EMOTION, IT'S TIME TO SURRENDER.

"IT'S NOT YOUR FAULT; IT WAS HIS TIME TO DEPART.
RELEASE YOUR BURDEN, IT WILL TEAR YOU APART.
WHEN LIFE GIVES SOMETHING HARD TO WITHSTAND
IT'S EASY TO BURY YOUR HEAD IN THE SAND.

"THESE FEELINGS ARE HEIGHTENED, NO CONTROL;
YOU ARE DIGGING YOURSELF A DEEPER HOLE.
WHEN SOMETHING IN LIFE HAS SUDDENLY GONE
YOU LEARN TO ADAPT FOR YOUR LIFE TO MOVE ON.

"IF A PERSON, HEALTH, OR POSSESSIONS YOU LOSE,
CONTINUE TO FIGHT FOR A LIFE THAT YOU CHOOSE.
YOU ARE NOT WEAK. LIFE IS NOT OVER.
YOU'RE IN CHARGE. MASTER AND CONTROLLER.

"BE STRONG, DETERMINED, AND WILLING TO DO
ALL THAT YOU NEED TO ENSURE YOU PULL THROUGH.
NOTHING MUST STOP YOU ACHIEVING POTENTIAL,
BE THE BEST YOU CAN BE — THAT'S THE ESSENTIAL."

FOX REGAINED COMPOSURE, HE FELT MUCH BETTER
HE THOUGHT BUTTERFLY WAS REALLY QUITE CLEVER.
"I NEED TO KNOW," FOX ASKED BUTTERFLY.
"WHY DID MY FATHER HAVE TO DIE?"

"EXPERIENCING LOSS MAKES YOU QUESTION,
YOU THINK, WONDER, AND PAY ATTENTION.
YOU QUESTION FUTURE, PRESENT AND PAST.
ONE THING YOU DISCOVER: NOTHING WILL LAST."

"ONE CERTAINTY IS WHAT IS BORN WILL DIE,
A LAW OF NATURE, YOU NEVER WILL DEFY.
NEVER FEAR DEATH, DEMISE IS INEVITABLE,
LIVE LIFE WELL, MAKE IT UNFORGETTABLE.

"LET'S GO INTO THE FOREST, I HAVE SOMETHING TO SHARE,
A WAY TO VIEW THINGS TO HELP YOU PREPARE."
FOX WALKED WITH BUTTERFLY FLYING AT HIS SIDE,
WONDERING WHAT REVELATIONS SHE WOULD PROVIDE.

DRIFTING THROUGH MEADOWS, AWASH WITH FLOWERS,
ADDRESSING MOTHER NATURE AND ALL OF HER POWERS.
BUTTERFLY LANDS ON A TREE FALLEN IN A STORM.
ALTHOUGH DECAYED, NEW SHOOTS ARE TAKING FORM.

"THE TREE'S LIFE IS OVER, WHAT'S LEFT IN ITS PLACE
THE ROOTS OF A NEW LIFE WHICH GROW TO REPLACE.
NOTHING IN NATURE DIES, THE LEGACY LIVES ON,
A PROCESS OF REPRODUCTION WHERE IT'S REBORN.

"MOTHER NATURE IS CONSTANTLY EVOLVING.
WHATEVER EARTH'S DILEMMA SHE'LL CONTINUE RESOLVING.
SHE WILL CREATE AND PRESERVE WITH INCREDIBLE BEAUTY,
AND TAKE IT AWAY IN A MOMENT OF CRUELTY.

"ALL THAT TRANSPIRES DURING THE PASSING OF TIME
IS RESTORED AND RECYCLED KEEPING LIFE AT ITS PRIME.
NATURE SURROUNDS YOU ALWAYS MAKING PROGRESS.
NATURE IS WITHIN YOU EVOLVING IN THE PROCESS.

"YOU ARE THE SUN, THE RAIN, THE WIND AND SNOW.
YOU ARE A CANYON, A MOUNTAIN AND A PLATEAU.
YOU ARE A CYCLONE, A HURRICANE AND A TORNADO.
YOU ARE A WATERFALL, A TIDAL WAVE AND A VOLCANO.

"YOU ARE A JUNGLE, A FOREST, A TREE AND A FLOWER.
YOU ARE NATURE ITSELF. YOU HAVE THE SAME POWER.
NATURE WILL GIVE, TAKE AND MAINTAIN.
A REFLECTION OF YOU, YOUR MIND AND YOUR BRAIN."

FOX WAS ENTHRALLED BY WHAT BUTTERFLY HAD SPOKEN,
HIS NATURAL INSTINCT HAD SUDDENLY AWOKEN.
FOX DECLARED, "I'M AS DIVERSE AS MOTHER NATURE.
A REPAIRER, DESTROYER AND A CREATOR.

"HOW DID YOU DISCOVER ALL OF THIS KNOWLEDGE?
DID YOU ATTEND A SCHOOL OR A COLLEGE?"
"FOX, THE WISDOM GAINED CAME FROM WITHIN
AND ALL THE EXPERIENCES LIFE CAN BRING.

"I WENT THROUGH THE PROCESS OF METAMORPHOSIS,
UNCOVERING THE DEPTH OF MY RESOURCEFULNESS.
FROM AN EGG, TO A CATERPILLAR, THEN A BUTTERFLY.
I NEEDED TO UNDERSTAND THE REASON WHY.

"EACH STAGE I LEARNT ABOUT ADAPTATION,
A MENTAL AND PHYSICAL TRANSFORMATION.
I HAD TO ADVANCE WITHOUT FEAR OF CHANGE,
FORCED UPON ME, DESPITE FEELING STRANGE.

"EACH CYCLE AN EXPERIENCE, A DIFFERENT ROLE,
A NATURAL PHENOMENON, UNABLE TO CONTROL.
I LEARNT ABOUT BIRTH, DEATH AND MEANING.
NOTHING EVER ENDS. IT'S SIMPLY A NEW BEGINNING.

"DEATH IS A VICTORY, IT'S NOT A DEFEAT,
ATTAIN WHAT IS VITAL TO MAKE LIFE COMPLETE.
WHEN A CYCLE IS OVER YOU BEGIN ANOTHER,
OLD CYCLES LEFT, FOR NEW ONES TO DISCOVER.

"EACH CYCLE IN LIFE PROVIDES SOMETHING NEW,
PROSPECTS, EXPERIENCE, A DIFFERENT POINT OF VIEW.
WHATEVER TRIAL YOU FACE, YOU MUST ENDURE,
YOU ACQUIRE KNOWLEDGE FOR YOU TO MATURE.

"LIKE A DIAMOND THAT NEEDS TO BE POLISHED,
FACETS GLEAMING, THEN LIFE IS ACCOMPLISHED.
YOUR SPIRIT WILL CONTINUE, THIS IS YOUR MIND.
CONNECT WITH YOUR SPIRIT, DON'T LEAVE IT BEHIND."

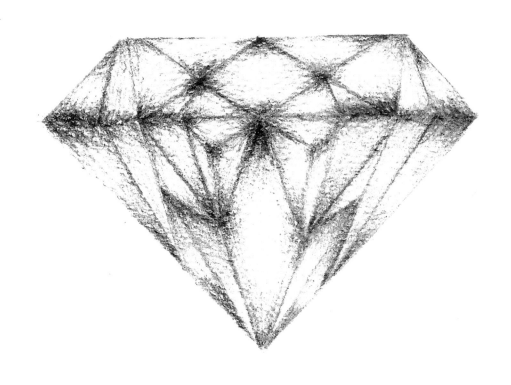

PONDERING WHAT BUTTERFLY HAD EXPLAINED,
"FATHER WAS A DIAMOND?" FOX PROCLAIMED.
FOX STOOD UP, YEARNING TO REJOICE
SHE HAD GONE, HE BARELY HEARD HER VOICE.

"CHANGE IS CONSTANT, FOX, ALWAYS PAY ATTENTION.
EXPECT THE UNEXPECTED, TO TAKE A NEW DIRECTION."
FOX WAS SHOCKED BY ALL SHE'D BEEN THROUGH,
WHAT SHE'D EXPLAINED HE FELT WAS ALL TRUE.

"I UNDERSTAND NATURE DID WHAT WAS NEEDED,
WITH EACH NEW CYCLE, YOU SUBMIT UNIMPEDED.
I MUST KEEP EVOLVING TO DEVELOP AND GROW.
I CAN'T LIVE IN THE PAST, I MUST LET IT GO."

"IT'S TIME, DEAR FOX, TO MOVE ON FROM THE PAIN,
YOUR FATHER'S LOVE WILL ALWAYS REMAIN.
HIS DEATH WAS TRAGIC BUT IT'S TIME TO RELEASE.
SCARS MAY REMAIN, YOU CAN NOW FEEL AT PEACE.

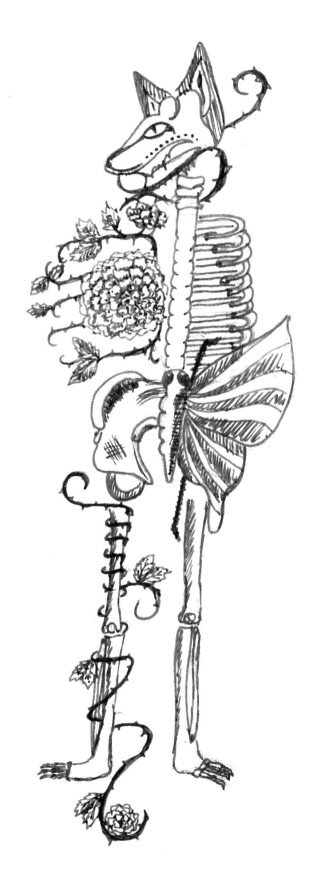

"REMEMBER, CHANGE IS CRUCIAL FOR LIFE'S SUCCESS.
A NATURAL PROCESS FOR YOU TO PROGRESS.
YOUR FATHER WOULD WANT YOU TO BE CONTENT,
LIVING LIFE TO THE FULL, ONE HUNDRED PER CENT."

"WHEN YOU NEED MY HELP, CALL MY NAME
I WILL OFFER THE GUIDANCE FOR YOU TO ATTAIN."
BUTTERFLY FLEW OFF TOWARDS MEADOWS OF GREEN.
FOX LOST SIGHT; SHE WAS NOWHERE TO BE SEEN.

THE NEXT DAY FOX TOOK A WALK BY THE RIVER.
WHAT BUTTERFLY HAD SAID WAS A LOT TO CONSIDER.
WITH A SENSE OF RELIEF SHE MADE HIM FEEL GOOD.
ALL THAT SHE SPOKE OF, FOX UNDERSTOOD.

THE GRIEF FOR HIS FATHER BEGAN TO DISAPPEAR.
THINGS IN HIS LIFE BEGAN TO FEEL CLEAR.
HE HAD MORE QUESTIONS TO ASK BUTTERFLY.
BUT FOR NOW FOX SAID A WARM GOODBYE.

THANK YOU TO

Sarah Kench and Cara Keeble at Chestnut Grove Academy for your time, patience and enthusiasm towards making this work.

To all the illustrators: for your vision. You created a world far greater than I could have ever imagined. Wishing you all huge success in your future endeavours. Dream big!

Akhera Williams   Talha Khan   Antonia Antrobus-Higgins

Kayley Hall   Tiarnan Matthews

Elisha Klimova   Hannah Butler   Isabella Gander

Gareth, Hayley, Lucy, Kate and Josh at Authoright for believing in this project.

Most of all to my late husband Hratch for all the knowledge shared. Our beautiful children are growing up to become remarkable individuals. You would be immensely proud of them.

All the doubters.... it's OK.... We just need to always believe that the impossible can happen!

THE MAKING OF AFTERLIFE:
A SCHOOL ART PROJECT

I feel so privileged that Tracy approached the art department at Chestnut Grove to help illustrate her story.

'Afterlife' so very beautifully deals with the complex feelings and emotions connected with bereavement and both the teachers and students felt incredibly moved by the story. It was a joy to illustrate; the pupils constantly inspired by the journey and the characters the fox meets along the way. Facilitating the collaboration process between Tracy and the students was a real pleasure and we thank Tracy for providing our students with a taste of what it is like to work as an illustrator. We hope Tracy and future readers enjoy the illustrations as much as we enjoyed creating them.

Miss Sarah Kench
Chestnut Grove Academy

www.chestnutgrove.wandsworth.sch.uk
www.twitter.com/ArtCga

QUOTES FROM OUR TALENTED STUDENT ARTISTS

'The story makes me think about the importance of life and that you should live life like there's no tomorrow. If they're gone you need to love but forget and forgive.' Kayley

'To come up with the ideas for my illustrations I found stanzas that resonated with me and literally drew what came to mind. The poetic words really assisted me in doing this.' Antonia

'My favourite part in the story is when the fox meets the other animals and all share their true belief in the meaning of life.' Elisha

'I love the fact the story is so metaphoric, it makes the narrative so relatable to so many different readers at once.' Alhera

'It was amazing being given a brief but yet having so much artistic freedom simultaneously.' Alhera

Lightning Source UK Ltd.
Milton Keynes UK
UKOW07f2006101116
287351UK00006B/34/P